T0198879

CAPTAIN UNITY

ROBERT DINO COMER

Captain "CU" Unity skits can be found at
www.robertdinocomerbooks.com.

To order additional copies of this book, contact:
Xlibris
844-714-8691
www.Xlibris.com
Orders@Xlibris.com

ISBN: 978-1-6698-7024-1 (sc)
ISBN: 978-1-6698-7025-8 (hc)
ISBN: 978-1-6698-7026-5 (e)

Library of Congress Control Number: 2023904499

Print information available on the last page

Rev. date: 02/15/2024

CAPTAIN UNITY

ROBERT "DINO" COMER

DEDICATION

I dedicate this book in memory of my mother
FANNIE JULIA THOMSON COMER
who gave me the sensitive strength, passion, and vision to
fight for good news no matter what disposition I am
facing in life.

Table of Contents

THE SET-UP
A Message from the Author on Why He Created

Captain "CU" Unity

This book guide was created because I believe that there is a familiar yet silent problem in our world that is lurking about. This problem does not have absolutely clear causes or easy solutions. This problem, this personal crime, is slowly eating away at society, at the very core of the spirit of humanity, especially our youth. This horrific disease is called *homelessness*!

Traditionally, *homelessness* is a *void*, defined as a physical state for any person, a child or a family, who does not have a secure home but is forced or by choice to live on the streets, such as sleeping inside and behind dumpsters, in alleys, under bridges, shelters, and inside abandoned houses and buildings.

Personally, I feel having the *void* of being *homeless* transcends our physical lives and easily permeate well beneath our skin. The void of being homeless is a mindset, a way of living and seeing oneself in the world that can settle in people mentally, emotionally, spiritually, and morally.

This is why I believe that the *void* of being *homeless* is not just an illness which plagues the poor and destitute. It can easily affect all, the very rich and powerful, the very creative and visionary trailblazers, just as easily as the average Joes and Joe-Zettes throughout society.

The *void* of being *homeless*, to its fullest, is no different from a person who is abusive or any form of bullying, to an elder, child, female, male, or any of God's defenseless creatures in a home, school, work, military, or the streets, as well as manipulating a person or a situation for their own selfish gain, as well as a person living a life of contradictions in order to say one thing and then change, only for their own selfish gain.

The *void* of being *homeless* is when a person gossips with the intention of belittling, degrading, or tearing down a person's heart, spirit, soul, mind, and character.

The *void* of being *homeless* is when a person has hatred and animosity in their heart toward others like racism and bigotry, as well as living their lives trying to make different types of people divisive toward one another.

The *void* of being *homeless* is when a person is constantly burning bridges, losing people close to them or people who had the possibility to become close to them.

The *void* of being *homeless* is a person who is dependent on drugs, alcohol, cigarettes, depression, gambling, or any destructive and excessive crutch, like food and shopping, to get them through their day-to-day existence.

And speaking of existing, the being *void* of *homeless* is a person who is merely existing in life and not living life.

But most importantly, the *void* being of *homeless* is no different from being a thief, and no, I am not simply talking about a person who steals from others, but a person who steals from themselves and do not realize that anything is missing!

That is what this book guide and website companion is all about.

You see, it is more than turning your head and walking in another direction when you see a person who looks to you like they have no home or shelter, but they are coming to you seeking honest, positive, and genuine help.

INTRODUCTION

Captain "CU" Unity is an interactive and educational book guide for peer mediation and conflict resolution. The concept of this project and its audience are created for all ages, nationalities, cultures, sexes, gender, faiths, and religions. This is a detailed audience for this project for grades 4 through 12, higher education (colleges and universities), social service establishments (juvenile detention centers, churches), government/military, franchises and startups, grassroot projects. This project is being shared through live performances via public and private performances, television, and through all Internet-based platforms. All themes and concepts are the original works of Robert "Dino" Comer.

INSPIRATION

Top: Fannie Julia Thompson Comer (mother)
Seated left to right: Susan Martin (aunt), Mary Sue Martin (grandma), Sharon Martin (aunt)
Front and center: Robert "Dino" Comer

Ma, how do you talk to people with respect?

My mom would ask me that question when I was just a kid. My mom said, "Dino, don't ever talk over anyone. Don't ever talk down to anyone. Talk to everyone eye to eye! Don't use big words or phrases unnecessarily. That way, your heart, soul, spirit, and mind will be understood and appreciated by anyone, no matter what walk of life they come from."

I took a moment and looked deep into my mother's eyes, hoping and praying I would somehow understand what she was saying. Hey, I was just a little fellow, remember? But unfortunately, I crawled away more puzzled than before I asked the question. But I must say, after a few "tappings" on my sensitive bottom, I began to understand how to talk to people with respect!

Thanks, Ma, for your tough, passionate, sensitive, and caring heart, not to mention your firm hand!

Soon after I learned that lesson, I created Captain "CU" Unity!

*The Birth of Captain **"CU" Unity**.*
Original childhood illustrations of what inspired the book

Spoiler alert: *After I ran up the fire escape, my goal was to end the evening by standing on top of the building, looking over the community. But I never made it because my mother would holler out just before I got to the top of the building, "Dino, get down here this very second . . . You have a spelling test first thing in the morning, and I want us to go over the words before you go to bed! And I mean now!"*

WHO IS *CAPTAIN "CU" UNITY?*

*Captain "C**U**" Unity Represents all ages, nationalities, cultures, disabilities, sexes, genders, faiths, and religions.*

*Captain "C**U**" Unity*
Has one parent.

*Captain "C**U**" Unity*
Has no parents.

*Captain "C**U**" Unity*
Is dirt poor.

*Captain "C**U**" Unity*
Is richer than rich.

*Captain "C**U**" Unity*
Is smack dab in the middle (class).

But most of all . . .
*Captain "C**U**"Unity is **us**.*

Have you ever created your own superhero? What is his or her name?

1. *If you have, please draw a picture below of how your superhero looks. If you haven't, please take the time now and draw a picture above of how you would like for your superhero to look.*
2. *Please write down what superpowers your superhero has and how he or she helps people.*

ACKNOWLEDGMENT

Before I begin to give my acknowledgements, I know I will forget some people. I am admitting this up front because I am not perfect. But I tried. In fact, my acknowledgment section may just be record-breaking. I mean, I have read a lot of books, but I don't think I have ever seen a book with as many acknowledgements that will be in this book. But of course, I will run into someone who will say to me in sadness or disgust, "Man, how could you forget about me? I changed your diapers when you were a baby," or "I helped you with your homework all through the first grade!" And I can say, "You're right! But keep in mind, I tried!" So to show how sensitive I am to include everybody I can, I will have an acknowledgment page on my companion website. So every time I think of someone I forgot or when someone brings it to my attention, I will quickly add them to my companion website acknowledgment page. Would you take that as fair? I guess I can take that as an OK!

So in advance, I would like to say right now I thank and appreciate everyone I have forgotten to put into the book!

So here it goes . . .

With such a vivid heartfelt longing, I can remember so passionately at the age of five years old my mother, *Fannie Julia Thompson Comer*, teaching me valuables lessons that any child could embrace, nurture, and share, as well as preparing me to face my life's journey as a teenager to adulthood; the prism of love, joy, happiness, and peace of mind or bestowing sensitive strength and humble passion to battle the bowls of pain, sorrow, disappointment, and heartache. My mother gave me sensitive strength, passion, and vision to fight for "good news," no matter what disposition I am facing in life.

My mother taught me to treat every age, nationality, culture, disability, sex, gender, faith, and religion as if I was them.

I soon learned that one of the greatest gifts I developed was having the sensitive strength and humble passion to break down barriers between any person that I meet so that I could feel comfortable and secure to communicate with anyone and not feel threatened or bullied. I thank, appreciate, and value those teachings from my mother as well as instilling in me to feel free and secure through the education of books and street wise common sense to communicate with anyone, especially the youth, my peers. These are just some of how *Captain "CU" Unity* was created by a little five-year-old inner-city kid from the drug-infested steel mill town of Gary, Indiana.

I have always practiced these beliefs. My mother felt all people's core existence was toward hope for a better tomorrow, and for that, I am honored and feel privileged to be afforded this opportunity to share that. It took a tapestry of masterly creative, gifted, talented, wise, and selfless humanity, especially our youth, some have loved, respected, and befriended me, and others simply tolerating me, but nevertheless, each and every one played a major part in some part of my journey to create and present *Captain "CU" Unity* to the world!

But one of the most valued lessons I learned growing up was my mother instilling in me that "no person is an island!"

1. To *Matthew Wisotsky*, associate director at Wayne State University Library System, Metro Detroit Michigan. Matt, it was you who made my dream book, *Captain "CU" Unity* a reality. With the deepest of sincere and honest emotions, I wish to offer consummate gratitude to you, Matt, for taking fifty years of my heart, vision, and passion and labor to help me create *Captain "CU" Unity* to be shared with the world, particularly our youth. Matt, not only are you a dear friend, but also a brother I wish I always had.

2. I truly thank and appreciate you, *"Momma" Deborah Wisotsky* and *Brother Matt Wisotsky*, for your selfless friendship and love during the time I was facing horrific hardship, physically, emotionally, mentally, and spiritually! "Momma" Wisotsky and Brother Matt, both of you are gifts from God! Both of you helped take me out of darkness and into the light!

3. I would like to take this moment to say that *Ms. Kara Cardeno*, my senior publishing consultant with Xlibris Publishing, is a consummate professional in true customer service! Ms. Cardeno is sincerely caring, understanding, and patient to my vision in my book dream, *Captain "CU" Unity*!" Xlibris Publishing is extremely lucky to have Ms. Cardeno as a team player! Ms. Cardeno is a "gift from God," and I'm blessed to have her intelligence, knowledge, and creativity in fighting tirelessly to make my book dream, *Captain "CU" Unity* a positive and productive success in helping humanity, especially our youth, through "peer mediation and conflict resolution"! I thank and appreciate you, Ms. Kara Cardeno!

4. I dedicate this jingle I created, entitled "The Inspirational Disability Law Group Jingle," to *Atty. Mandy Kelly/The Disability Law Group*, for fighting tirelessly in a positive, creative, and productive way, when the John D. Dingell VA Medical Center/US Department of Veterans Affairs continued to ignore, walk away, and deny me, a soldier who served the United States Army with distinguished honorable status, for the mental, emotional, and physical disease I have been facing for approximately thirty-eight years! In fact, an employee at the Patrick V. McNamara Federal Building told me I was stupid if I chose a law firm to Fight for me when I became disenchanted with the lack of support and care they gave me, even when I had faced homelessness and manic depression throughout my entire time/life when I got out of service! I said, why would I be stupid? They said I would have to give the law firm a percentage. I said I'd rather get 80 percent of something than a 100 percent of nothing! I would like to give a special shout-out to Ms. Elyse Faulk, office manager under Ms. Mandy Kelly/The Disability Law Group, for all the hard work and honesty you gave me as you did research and fought for me! I thank and appreciate both of you, Ms. Mandy Kelly and Ms. Elyse Faulk, for never giving up on me and winning my service-connected disability claim so that I can now stop "sleepwalking through life" and now have some "peace of mind as I continue my journey in life!"

Now for the jingle!

"The Inspirational Disability Law Group Jingle"

Created and written on November 25, 2019
By Robert Louis "Dino" Comer Jr.

Sit back, relax, us, veterans, don't want any mess
because we've got something we want to express.

We've heard every jingle from A to Z,
but we've never heard a jingle about the
Disability Law Group, you see.

It's one of the greatest law firms that exist,
fighting tirelessly for your Social Security disability,
with veteran pension benefits topping the list.

The Disability Law Group's goal is to fight for us, vets,
because we are risking our lives to serve our country
as well as honoring the vets who lay in rest.

So, vets, reach out to the Disability Law Group and don't think twice
because they will help you and your family stop
"existing" and start "living life"!

And if you don't believe what we've said true,
Just call Atty. Mandy Kelly at 248-838-3000
and see what she can do for you.

5. I thank and appreciate you, *Prof. Fred J. Florkowski*, associate professor, director of theatre and scenic design at Maggie Allesee Department of Theatre and Dance at Wayne State University, Detroit, Michigan, for not only having been my academic advisor and mentor, but most importantly, as well as an unconditional friend! Professor Fred, you've made making *Captain "CU" Unity* a much easier and enjoyable journey!

6. I thank and appreciate *Ms. Audrey Kates Bailey*, who, at the time in 1985, was the program development officer for North Carolina's statewide public television network, reaching over two million viewers within the North Carolina, South Carolina, Tennessee, Virginia, and Georgia PBS/public TV viewership, for giving me the opportunity to perform a one-hour educational and innovative motivational presentation, entitled "Dropping the Knowledge," and subsequently, two educational and innovative vignettes, "Sony's Revenge" and "It's a Steal," which teach peer mediation and conflict resolutions, which received critical acclaim.

7. I thank and appreciate *Paramount Station Group Fox 22 (WLFL) TV (Raleigh, Durham, Fayetteville) children's show Pizzazz* for giving me the position as cohost and head writer for *Pizzazz*. Various segments from some of the *Pizzazz* shows will be vignettes in *Captain "CU" Unity*!

8. I thank and appreciate *Ms. Helen Dickens*/North Carolina Department of Transportation who gave me the opportunity to be a part of the creating process as the cowriter of the "North Carolina Department of Transportation's Educational Engineering Video Rap Short and Host," which successfully reaches millions of youth internationally. This educational engineering video rap short will be presented in *Captain "CU" Unity*!

9. I thank and appreciate *Rowell Gormon*, a man with 999 and 1/2 voices/voices2go.com, for his selfless technically creative imagination and his visionary voices for "Sonee's Revenge" and "It's a Steal." And now "Sonees's Revenge" and "It's a Steal" will be presented in *Captain "CU" Unity*

10. I thank and appreciate my mother, and I love you, *Ms. Martha Keravuori*, former executive director of the North Carolina conference for your trueness in showing consummate love to my mother and me. We thank and appreciate you for being our friend and finding journeys for me to grow as an educational entertainer to humanity, especially our youth, in the beginning of my career. Now, Ms. Keravuori, that beginning is in the present. I thank and appreciate you!

11. I thank and appreciate *Ms. Belinda Black Brodie*, former administrator for North Carolina Department of Public Instruction's School Television. If it wasn't for you and Ms. Audrey, my vision presented through *Captain "CU" Unity* would never be a reality. I thank and appreciate you, Ms. Belinda, for incorporating some of my motivational, entertaining, and educational vignettes into the daytime broadcast schedule for North Carolina Department of Public Instruction's School Television.

12. I thank and appreciate *Jim Vidakovich*, People's Center Management and former producer of the Sesame Workshop, formerly the Children's Television Workshop. It's this simple: Mr. Vidakovich, you are a "consummate concierge" in the field of educational entertainment. I was given the opportunity to be introduced to Mr. Vidakovich, subsequently, when he selected me with five other

actors, out of six hundred actors who competed to become professional children's actors for "Kaiser Permanente's Professional Children's Touring Show" (Professor Body), which was produced on a national scale. This was my introduction to educate and entertain humanity, especially our youth, on peer mediation and conflict resolution.

13. I thank and appreciate **Wake County Public School System**, Raleigh, North Carolina, for giving me the opportunity to use my gifts and talents to educate humanity, especially our youth, through entertaining by getting hands-on experience in educating through teaching. It was such a wealth of journeyed knowledge as a substitute teacher for seven years in Wake County Public School System, with duties as acting on behalf of absent class instructors and being able to advance scheduled lesson plans, administer test, devise and supervise appropriate activities in specific instructions for K-12.

14. I thank and appreciate *Bruce and Iteena Williams* and *Charles Eric and Alice Peschl Swain* for their friendship.

Chapter 1

Attack Life with Your Heart

Everyone Has a Copyright in Their Heart

Please visit www.robertdinocomerbooks.com
to view content related to the following discussion prompts.

1. What is your copyright dream(s)?

2. What steps are you taking to make your copyright dream(s) come true?

Lift Up Your Head and Smile

Please visit www.robertdinocomerbooks.com
to view content related to the following discussion prompts.

1. What does "lift up your head and smile" mean to you?

2. Who are the people you can say you dedicate your life to at this point of your life right now and why?

Health Care
for All
Humanity

*Please visit www.robertdinocomerbooks.com
to view content related to the following discussion prompts.*

1. What do you think "health care for all humanity" means?

2. Do you give health care to everyone you come into contact with? How do you show it, or what are some ways you show it?

Chapter 2

The Art of Respect

Sonee's Revenge

Please visit www.robertdinocomerbooks.com
to view content related to the following discussion prompts.

1. Have you ever disrespected someone's property and why?

2. Have you ever disrespected someone in any way and why?

Clean Up
Your Act
First

Please visit www.robertdinocomerbooks.com
to view content related to the following discussion prompts.

1. What does it mean to " clean up your own act first"?

2. Why should you clean up your own act first before you work on your goals and dreams?

Female
Abuse
101

*Please visit www.robertdinocomerbooks.com
to view content related to the following discussion prompts.*

1. Why is it important for all males to stand beside and support females?

2. How can males support females even when the females are wrong?

Chapter 3

Hey, It's All U phill

Don't Be Afraid to Think, It's Not Illegal Yet!

Please visit www.robertdinocomerbooks.com
to view content related to the following discussion prompts.

1. What does it mean to "think because it's not illegal yet"?

2. Why should you think first before you take any action?

Knock You Down, You Get Up

Please visit www.robertdinocomerbooks.com to view content related to the following discussion prompts.

18

1. If you get knocked down, what ways would you fight to get up?

Label "Me" Not: Part 1

Please visit www.robertdinocomerbooks.com
to view content related to the following discussion prompts.

Label "Me" Not: Part 2

Please visit www.robertdinocomesbooks.com
to view content related to the following discussion prompts.

Part 1: Do you think it's hurtful to label someone, especially our youth, and why?

Part 2: What do you think it means when it is says that there are more important things to do than to watch the news, the TV, just in general, playing video games for many hours of the day, or just being on the Internet or having full access to it before you take any action?

Chapter 4

Turning Negatives into Positives

The Adventures of Captain Unity

Please visit www.robertdinocomesbooks.com
to view content related to the following discussion prompts.

1. Why must you stand up and defend yourself and everyone else who is being abused by the "calling people bad name villain"?

2. And how would you do it?

Positive Stealing: Part 1

Please visit www.robertdinocomerbooks.com
to view content related to the following discussion prompts.

Positive Stealing: Part 2

Please visit www.robertdinocomerbooks.com
to view content related to the following discussion prompts.

1. How would you tell someone who steals from themselves that it is one of the greatest crimes they are committing?

Taking Care of Your Garden First

*Please visit www.robertdinocomerbooks.com
to view content related to the following discussion prompts.*

1. Why do you think it is important to take care of your own garden before you even think of someone else's garden?

One Bullet, One Life

Please visit www.robertdinocomerbooks.com
to view content related to the following discussion prompts.

1. What does " you are not a cat and you don't have nine lives" mean to you?

2. How would you tell someone, no matter how they are feeling and no matter what they are going through, that they should not take a person's life?

Chapter 5

The Creativity Within

G W
Fashion

Please visit www.robertdinocomerbooks.com
to view content related to the following discussion prompts.

1. What does economic empowerment mean to you?

2. How would you use economic empowerment no matter where you are in life?

Be the Best Garbage Person You Can Be

Please visit www.robertdinocomerbooks.com to view content related to the following discussion prompts.

1. What does " being the best garbage person you can be" mean to you?

2. What is the best "garbage person" you want to be, and how are you going to be about to becoming it?

An Apple a Day, Keeps Your Dreams Alive

Please visit www.robertdinocomerbooks.com
to view content related to the following discussion prompts.

1. What is your apple a day, and how do and how are or do you keep it alive?

Chapter 6

The Magic of Education

The Power of Reading: Part 1

Please visit www.robertdinocomerbooks.com
to view content related to the following discussion prompts.

The Power of Reading: Part 2

Please visit www.robertdinocomerbooks.com
to view content related to the following discussion prompts.

Part 1: Why is it fun and exciting to read?

Part 2: Why is it important to read about things you don't like or even hate?

The Art of Selling Math, Science, and Engineering Like a New Drug

Please visit www.robertdinocomerbooks.com
to view content related to the following discussion prompts.

1. How would you go about selling math, science, and engineering like people selling drugs to our youth so that it will equal to success to our youth?

About the Author

Robert "Dino" Comer

Author, entertainer, youth advocate, social and medical philanthropist, Army veteran of honorable status, has a diverse, passionate, and innovative approach to successful creative practices in the field of peer mediation and conflict resolution. With three decades as an educational visionary, Dino has had his gifts and talents tapped into by being requested to create, consult, write, produce, direct, lecture, and conduct workshops to a diverse group of *Fortune* 500 companies, educational institutions (from kindergarten to higher education), federal and state agencies, United States Army, television and radio media outlets, and various religious outlets.

All Dino's books and more information
and fun can be found at
www.robertdinocomerbooks.com.

Printed in the United States
by Baker & Taylor Publisher Services